BASEBALL LEGENDS

Hank Aaron
Grover Cleveland Alexander
Ernie Banks
Albert Belle
Johnny Bench
Yogi Berra
Barry Bonds
Roy Campanella
Roberto Clemente
Ty Cobb
Dizzy Dean
Joe DiMaggio
Bob Feller
Jimmie Foxx
Lou Gehrig
Bob Gibson
Ken Griffey, Jr.
Rogers Hornsby
Walter Johnson
Sandy Koufax
Greg Maddux
Mickey Mantle
Christy Mathewson
Willie Mays
Stan Musial
Satchel Paige
Mike Piazza
Cal Ripken, Jr.
Brooks Robinson
Frank Robinson
Jackie Robinson
Babe Ruth
Tom Seaver
Duke Snider
Warren Spahn
Willie Stargell
Frank Thomas
Honus Wagner
Ted Williams
Carl Yastrzemski
Cy Young

Chelsea House Publishers

BASEBALL LEGENDS

ALBERT BELLE

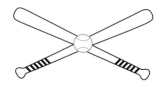

Dennis R. Tuttle

Introduction by
Jim Murray

Senior Consultant
Earl Weaver

CHELSEA HOUSE PUBLISHERS
Philadelphia

Produced by Choptank Syndicate, Inc.

Editor and Picture Researcher: Norman L. Macht
Production Coordinator and Editorial Assistant: Mary E. Hull
Designer: Lisa Hochstein
Cover Design: Alison Burnside
Cover Photo Credit: AP/Wide World Photo

CONTENTS

WHAT MAKES A STAR

Jim Murray

No one has ever been able to explain to me the mysterious alchemy that makes one man a .350 hitter and another player, more or less identical in physical makeup, hard put to hit .200. You look at an Al Kaline, who played with the Detroit Tigers from 1953 to 1974. He was pale, stringy, almost poetic-looking. He always seemed to be struggling against a bad case of mononucleosis. But with a bat in his hands, he was King Kong. During his career, he hit 399 home runs, rapped out 3,007 hits, and compiled a .297 batting average.

Form isn't the reason. The first time anybody saw Roberto Clemente step into the batter's box for the Pittsburgh Pirates, the best guess was that Clemente would be back in Double A ball in a week. He had one foot in the bucket and held his bat at an awkward angle—he looked as though he couldn't hit an outside pitch. A lot of other ballplayers may have had a better-looking stance. Yet they never led the National League in hitting in four different years, the way Clemente did.

Not every ballplayer is born with the ability to hit a curveball. Nor is exceptional hand-eye coordination the key to heavy hitting. Big league locker rooms are filled with players who have all the attributes, save one: discipline. Every baseball man can tell you a story about a pitcher who throws a ball faster than anyone has ever seen but who has no control on or *off* the field.

The Hall of Fame is full of people who transformed themselves into great ballplayers by working at the sport, by studying the game, and making sacrifices. They're overachievers—and winners. If you want to find them, just watch the World Series. Or simply read about New York Yankee great Lou Gehrig; Ted Williams, "the Splendid Splinter" of the Boston Red Sox; or the Dodgers' strikeout king Sandy Koufax.

A pitcher *should* be able to win a lot of ballgames with a 98-miles-per-hour fastball. But what about the pitcher who wins 20 games a year with a fastball so slow that you can catch it with your teeth? Bob Feller of the Cleveland Indians got into the Hall of Fame with a blazing fastball that glowed in the dark. National League star Grover Cleveland Alexander got there with a pitch that took considerably longer to reach the plate; but when it did arrive, the pitch was exactly where Alexander wanted it to be—and the last place the batter expected it to be.

There are probably more players with exceptional ability who didn't make it to the major leagues than there are who did. A number of great hitters, bored with fielding practice, had to be dropped from their team because their home-run production didn't make up for their lapses in the field. And then there are players like Brooks Robinson of the Baltimore Orioles, who made himself into a human vacuum cleaner at third base because he knew that working hard to become an expert fielder would win him a job in the big leagues.

A star is not something that flashes through the sky. That's a comet. Or a meteor. A star is something you can steer ships by. It stays in place and gives off a steady glow; it is fixed, permanent. A star works at being a star.

And that's how you tell a star in baseball. He shows up night after night and takes pride in how brightly he shines. He's Willie Mays running so hard his hat keeps falling off; Ty Cobb sliding to stretch a single into a double; Lou Gehrig, after being fooled in his first two at-bats, belting the next pitch off the light tower because he's taken the time to study the pitcher. Stars never take themselves for granted. That's why they're stars.

1

A SUPER YEAR

"When they coined the term tunnel vision, they had Albert in mind."
— Mike Hargrove, Indians manager

In 1995, the Cleveland Indians rewarded their long-suffering fans by reaching the World Series for the first time since 1954. They went 100–44, and if the players' strike had not shortened the season by 18 games, they would have had a chance at the American League record of 111 victories set by that '54 team.

Like all great teams, one player served as its enforcer, the player every opponent feared. That player in Cleveland was left fielder and power hitter Albert Belle.

"There's nobody in here who wants to produce more than he does," said catcher Sandy Alomar. "Nobody wants to win more. He's just very intense."

With his short, compact swing that sprayed line drives to all fields, Belle intimidated pitchers with his bat as much as his scowl. He came to the batter's box skulking, glaring and daring the pitcher to challenge him. He was so determined to be perfect that he once hit a home run, rounded the bases and then rushed to the underground batting cage. He was furious at himself for not hitting the home run pitch as solidly as he thought he should.

Albert Belle sees every pitcher as the enemy, and steps into the batter's box daring the enemy to throw the ball. From 1991 through 1996, Belle hit 186 home runs, the most in the major leagues.

"When they coined the term tunnel vision, they had Albert in mind," said Indians manager Mike Hargrove.

"He looks at the game as a battle," said one of his best friends on the team, clubhouse attendant Frank Mancini. "It's war. Anybody who's not on his team is against him. That's the enemy."

From 1991 to 1995, there was not a more productive player. Belle's 186 home runs were the most in the major leagues. His 563 runs batted in were second to the 564 by Frank Thomas of the Chicago White Sox. And his .588 slugging percentage was second only to Barry Bonds of San Francisco.

Belle hit 30 or more homers for five consecutive seasons. In the strike-shortened 1994 season, he batted .357 with 36 homers and 101 RBI. If so many games had not been lost to the strike, Belle would have had a good chance to break Roger Maris's record of 61 homers in a full season and win the triple crown of home run, RBI and batting titles.

"I don't know about that," Belle said. "But no matter how many home runs I hit, no matter how many runs I drive in, it's not as important as winning the World Series. I'd give up any personal accomplishment for that World Series ring."

Belle and the Indians wasted little time striving for that goal in 1995. They started the season 46-21, and it wasn't Belle who had triggered their league-leading offense. He batted a respectable .312 with 14 homers and 51 RBI in the first half. However, Kenny Lofton, Manny Ramirez, Jim Thome and Eddie Murray, along with the league's best pitching staff, helped the

Indians to a 12-game lead in the AL Central Division at the All-Star break.

But Belle exploded and had one of the best second halves in history. He batted .322 with 36 homers, 75 RBI and 25 doubles. He had a 15-game hitting streak in August, seven two-homer games and two three-homer games in the final two months. His 17 home runs in September tied Babe Ruth's record for most homers in a month. And when he collected his 50th double on Sept. 17 against Boston and his

Although Hank Aaron hit more home runs in his career—755—and Roger Maris hit more in one season—61, all modern sluggers are still chasing the ghost of Babe Ruth, who averaged over 50 home runs a year for six years. Nobody else has ever come close.

50th homer Sept. 30 against Kansas City, he became the first player to reach 50 doubles and 50 homers in a season.

"All the great home run hitters, all the great batting champions, and I'm the only one to have done that?" Belle said with great pride. "That amazes me. To put your name on a record like that is really gratifying."

Belle finished the season with a .317 batting average, 50 homers, 126 RBI, 121 runs and 52 doubles in just 143 games. He led the league in homers, total bases, runs, doubles, slugging percentage and extra-base hits, and seemed a shoo-in to be the league's most valuable player, especially since the Indians won the AL Central by a record 30 games over the White Sox. But Boston first baseman Mo Vaughn won the honor by eight votes.

Cleveland fans were outraged. How could a player have one of the best offensive seasons in history, lead his team to the World Series, and not win the MVP?

Vaughn had a lower batting average (.300), fewer home runs (39), and tied Belle for the RBI lead (126). The Red Sox won fewer games and were even swept in the first round of the play-offs by the Indians.

"It seems like every year when it comes to the MVP voting there is a different issue," Belle said. "One year Cecil Fielder hits 50 home runs. Well, he played on a last-place team. So this year, I hit 50 home runs, but I had a team full of MVPs. There are a lot of different arguments, but as far as an everyday position player, based on what I've done on the field, there shouldn't be any competition as far as MVP voting."

But the writers who did the voting remembered another side of Belle: how he thrived on his anger, how he refused to talk to reporters during the season, how he was constantly warned and reprimanded for his temper tantrums toward opposing players and fans.

He was suspended five times in five seasons for throwing a ball at a fan, charging the mound, using a corked bat, abusing reporters, and attempting to injure another player. Because of his temper he became a marked man, the type everyone picked on because they knew he would explode. He was called selfish and sinister.

The people close to Belle said he was dedicated, hard-working, smart, educated and talented, but very complex. He was great with charities and children. "He is the most popular athlete in Cleveland," said general manager John Hart. "They love him. He's been with us through the ups and downs of the franchise, and he's a big part of the community."

But when he lost the MVP award, newspaper articles throughout the country said Belle got what he deserved for being such a bully. Once again, it seemed, he was paying for the behavior and reputation that had followed him since he was a little boy growing up in Shreveport, Louisiana.

2

A FAMILY'S LOVE

"You couldn't ask for nicer boys. They said, 'yes sir and no sir' and they respected everyone so much."
— Gene Procell, Little League coach

Albert JoJuan Belle was born August 25, 1966, in Shreveport, Louisiana, four minutes before his brother, Terry. They were the only children of Albert and Carrie Belle, and they were typical middle-class boys who were taught the importance of studying hard, attending church, respecting their parents and peers, and striving to do their very best in everything they did.

The boys' disciplined home life centered around their Baptist parents, both of whom were teachers. Their mother taught math and their father was a football and baseball coach. The boys were raised to understand the importance of working hard and never settling for second best. Whether it was video games, sports, school or church, the boys grew up hating to fail. Joey, as Albert was called throughout his childhood and early adult life, was especially focused and determined to be the very best. "The Belles were video fanatics," said high school friend and baseball teammate Byron Copeland. "They had played Ms. Pac-Man so much trying to master the game that they had the pat-

Gene Procell coached the Belle brothers' Little League team, the Saints. In two years the Saints won 30 games and lost 2. The team hit a lot of home runs, but, says Procell, "What separated Joey from all the other boys was how smart he was."

terns figured out to the point that they could play an hour on one quarter."

The brothers became as competitive and determined in their school work as in their sports and games. They loved playing chess, Ping-Pong and basketball. But most of all, they loved to read. "Books were always important," Terry said. "We couldn't go out of the house in the summer until 12 o'clock—after we had done our reading.

"We won lots of awards from the summer reading program. We loved autobiographies," Terry added. "We wouldn't go to sleep until one had outread the other. Like if I got up in the middle of the night to go to the bathroom or something, I'd check to see what page [his] marker was on. If it was page 207, then I'd read to page 227 so that when he woke up the next morning, I'd be ahead of him."

The hours of hard studying paid off for the brothers. As a senior in high school, Joey was a class officer, member of the National Honor Society, and vice president of the Future Business Leaders of America. He was also named one of the outstanding high school athletes in the country. Terry was also a member of the National Honor Society, and president of the Fellowship of Christian Athletes. Joey ranked sixth in a class of 266 at Huntington High School and Terry seventh. Both were whizzes in math and both studied accounting at Louisiana State University. After college Terry got his Master's degree and became a financial analyst. But, Terry confessed, "My brother is better at math than me."

"They were very motivated in their school work," said high school baseball coach Phillip Williams.

As kids, the brothers also became Eagle Scouts and junior deacons at church. "They made good grades, they attended church, and at that time church came before baseball," said Mike Spence, one of their summer league coaches. "If we had a Sunday baseball game, they were at church. I made sure they didn't miss too many games because we didn't schedule many Sunday games."

"I'm speaking for Terry also when I say this," Joey said when he was in high school. "We put God first in our lives. We go to church every Wednesday and Sunday. We feel good about ourselves and good in games because we know the Lord is with us."

"I am a proud mother because my sons have their priorities straight with spiritual activity first, academics second and sports third," Carrie Belle said.

The Belles' home life was so structured around respect for others that "I don't even recall Joey and Terry ever being in a situation where their parents had to get on them," Williams said. "They have a very good mom and dad. They are very good people. Very intellectual people and very disciplined. The boys would come to my house, and I lived out in the country, and they had to call mom and dad to say where they were. They were very good kids."

"You couldn't ask for nicer boys," said Gene Procell, who coached them in Little League baseball at ages 11 and 12. "They said, 'yes sir and no sir' and they respected everyone so much. Their daddy helped me coach and I'd bring the team to my house and give them some hot dogs. Joey and Terry always appreciated that and always told me thank you."

Belle and his brother spent many hours each week in the old Galilee Baptist Church before the church moved to a new building in 1975. His minister, Rev. Edward Jones, recalls that Joey "had a temper that was pretty high" when he was young.

Both parents were very good athletes. And thanks to the patience and attention of their father, the boys developed a deep love and respect for sports. Albert Belle was an assistant coach at Airline High School, one of the top baseball programs in the country. He would often throw them 100 pitches in batting practice. "He taught us how to hit, catch and throw in the front yard when we were seven," Terry said. "When we went to Minnesota for mother's surgery, daddy used to take us out to the park and we would practice hitting. We also saw a lot of softball games and we liked them."

"They were driven to be good and they loved it that way," said Jim Wells, who coached them in youth and college baseball. "Coach Belle would stay out there for hours throwing batting prac-

tice and hitting them fly balls. Every time you ever saw them it was Joey, Terry and their dad."

"More than anything, Joey worked for what he had," said coach Spence. "Even as a kid, he didn't say, 'I'm a good ballplayer' and that's the end of it. He worked hard. More kids need to be like that."

But a baseball player will always make more outs than hits. Joey had a hard time accepting this fact of the game. He would get angry and throw bats or batting helmets. "I brought him up to excel at everything," his mother explained. "He wants to be perfect."

Some people said the Belles' parents were too protective of them and placed too much pressure on them to excel. Although the boys were well-behaved, there were early signs that Joey's drive for perfection would become his worst enemy.

"We're more aware of who the kid really is," said his minister at Galilee Baptist Church, the Rev. Edward Jones. "He was a very quiet and humble boy. One thing we did note . . . was he had a real focus on winning. He had a temper that was pretty high and he would go on tirades even then because he was so focused on what he was doing."

Outstanding Player
JOEY BELLE
Huntington

3

INTELLIGENCE
AT THE PLATE

"The reason he made it was his love for the game and his work ethic."
— Jim Wells, coach, University of Alabama

Like most boys who grow up to be major-leaguers, little Joey Belle was a very good athlete and an exceptional baseball player. In the Dixie Youth Little League, he played center field and shortstop and pitched, and he also hit a lot of home runs. His team, the Saints, went 30–2 in two years, and they were so good that many of their games didn't go the full six innings because of the 10-run slaughter rule. They went 16–0 when the boys were 12 years old; often games on the other fields had to be stopped to get the home run balls that Joey and his teammates had hit.

"In the Dixie Youth All-Star game, at the age of 12, I hit a winning, two-out grand slam in the bottom of the last inning and we won the game, 6–3," Joey said proudly. But his team lost in the bi-district playoffs to Springhill, ending their undefeated season.

"Joey stood out because he hit a lot of home runs," said his coach, Gene Procell. "But what separated Joey from all other boys was how smart he was. He'd get up to that plate and he was all business. He really concentrated on the ball. He

Belle was an All-State pitcher/outfielder for two years at Huntington High School in Shreveport, Louisiana. In 1984 his brother, Terry, also made the All-State team.

didn't fool around and you could see it on his face. He studied every pitch and if it was in a spot he didn't like, he wouldn't swing at it. He'd hit the ball square and in full stride. If that pitcher threw him one on the outside part of the plate, he'd reach out and drive it into right field."

"He had great instincts," said Jim Wells, who coached the Belle brothers on two championship teams at ages 13 and 14. Wells, who later became head coach at the University of Alabama, recalled Joey being far superior to anyone else his age. "He definitely had some natural gifts, but the reason he made it was his love for the game and his work ethic."

The boys were such students of baseball that they would watch games on TV and pick up pointers. They knew all the players and read everything they could about baseball. They even read the rules book as though they were going to be umpires.

"When we were growing up his idols were Jim Palmer and Eddie Murray," Terry said. "Mine were Roberto Clemente and Dave Parker."

Joey and Terry were always challenging each other. "They were usually the two best players and they were usually competing against themselves to be the best," Wells said.

"They were hard on one another," said high school friend Byron Copeland. "Sometimes Terry would throw batting practice and if he threw two or three bad ones in a row, Joey would get on him. Joey had an incredible eye for the strike zone and even in practice he wouldn't swing at a bad pitch.

"They were always the first ones at the ballpark and the last ones to leave," Copeland added. "They practiced constantly. People talk about

Joey being great. But he was as focused of a practice player as anyone. When he and Terry got into the batting cage they would stay until dark every night."

The folks around Shreveport knew Joey was a great baseball player, but he began to get national attention when he was 15. Wells took him to a baseball camp at Oklahoma State University and "the coaches there made references that he was a big-time player," Wells said.

At Huntington High School, the boys also played football. Joey was the starting quarterback, free safety, and kicker. Terry played guard. Neither of the boys was especially big or fast, but they were good enough athletes to help Huntington tie for the district championship their junior year. As seniors, they lost to state power Ruston High, 28–27, in the first round of the playoffs.

Albert Belle visits with his Little League coach, Gene Procell, during a return to Shreveport. Procell had no problems with the 12-year-old Joey and Terry. "You couldn't ask for nicer boys," he said.

While it was no surprise that college recruiters didn't scout the boys as football players, it was surprising how few looked at them as baseball players. "Shreveport was a dry area," Copeland said. "At one point the town had been a good baseball town, but baseball was down in the years the Belles were playing, so not many scouts came through."

"That's true," said Louisiana State University coach Skip Bertman. "In those days, the competition level among Louisiana high school kids was so poor that many professional baseball teams didn't have scouts here. Louisiana baseball was very weak in high school. Like most southern states, Louisiana was predominantly a football state. It was a sign of the times. Because the lights were poor, the umpiring was poor, and the parks were in terrible shape, guys like Joey Belle didn't get any attention. But in a 10-year period after him, it was a warp-speed turnaround. Beautiful ballparks, more youth leagues, winter ball, better coaches. Guys like Belle made that happen."

In 1982, the boys' sophomore year, Huntington lost in the state quarterfinals despite Joey's home run. The next year, they lost in the second round of the state playoffs. As a pitcher,

The Belle brothers were the whole story in this 1984 semifinal win in the state playoffs. Joey hit a grand slam and pitched the complete game. Terry hit a two-run triple and walked twice.

Raiders win by the Belles

RUSTON — As long as Huntington's Belles (Joey and Terry) continue to chime, the Raiders will have a chance in the Class AAAA state baseball playoffs.

The Belles chimed again Wednesday as the twins combined to knock in seven Raider runs as Huntington whipped host Ruston, 9-7, in bidistrict action.

The Raiders (14-8) will now play District 2-AAAA champion Airline (17-6) in a game tentatively set for 4 p.m., today at Airline.

Terry, who was walked twice intentionally, got the Raiders rolling early as he delivered a two-run triple in the first to score Mitch Hanning (single) and Joey (walk).

Joey, a returning all-stater, then stole the spotlight in the second inning. Mike Harville led off the frame with a double, Ken Davidson walked and Hanning singled to load the bases. Joe Hughes followed with an RBI infield single.

Joey then crunched losing pitcher Barry Taylor's (8-3) fastball 375-feet over the right-center field fence for a grand slam and a 7-0 Huntington lead.

Ruston scored two runs in the second. The Bearcats loaded the bases with none out and designated hitter Karl Williamson stroked a two-run single.

Joey, who went the distance on the mound to run his record to 6-2, fanned the next batter and Huntington got a double play to end the threat.

Joey gave Huntington an 8-2 lead with an RBI-double off the center field fence in the fourth that scored Hughes (single). He now has 47 RBI for the year.

Ruston added three more in the sixth to pull within 8-5 on a throwing error by Joey, an RBI-groundout by Taylor and a sacrifice fly by Williamson. Huntington scored its final run when Robbie Rice tripled and Don Gibbs, a state high jumper, singled him in.

Kerry Merritt added a two-out, two-run inside-the-park homer over the left fielder's head in the seventh to give Ruston its final runs.

Joey struck out 10 and fanned Todd Anderson to end the Bearcat comeback hopes.

Ruston, the District 3-AAAA co-champion, ends the season 11-6.

Joey Belle

Joey was 6–3 with a 2.52 earned-run average. He also batted .643 with 37 runs batted in, 23 stolen bases, and had a 10-game hitting streak. Terry, a first baseman and outfielder, batted .414 with 21 RBI and had an 11-game hitting streak.

As juniors, the line-drive hitting Terry batted third and Joey batted fourth, and most teams pitched around Joey. So during their senior season, Joey batted third and Terry fourth. The result was immediate: Joey batted .633 with 8 home runs, 42 RBI and just two strikeouts in 67 at-bats to become the most valuable player on the all-city team. He was also 5–2 with a 1.14 ERA and 64 strikeouts in 43 innings as a pitcher. Terry batted .520 with 24 RBI.

Huntington lost the championship game, but Joey was named state co-MVP. Still, there was virtually no interest by the pros and little by colleges. Oklahoma State had remembered him from the camp he attended. Notre Dame gave him a look but Joey, used to warm spring seasons in Louisiana, was not impressed with baseball practices on 25-degree days.

During the summer after his senior year, Joey was picked for the USA National Junior baseball team that won a silver medal in the World Youth International Championships. Bertman, in his first year of coaching at LSU, believed both Belle brothers were worthy of partial scholarships. Those who had grown up with them and played with them could not disagree.

4

THE EMERGING STAR

"The truth of it is, he couldn't control himself."
— Skip Bertman, coach, LSU

It made perfect sense that Joey and Terry would attend college together and become roommates. No one could motivate one better than the other and they were also best friends. They entertained their dormitory and teammates with their good-natured joking, took the same classes, went to meals together, and practiced baseball together.

Terry found little playing time as a freshman and sophomore, but Joey showed such dramatic improvement from his fall freshman season that he won a starting job in the spring. He worked on his hitting, especially driving the ball to the opposite field, and he began a weight-lifting program that helped him gain strength for a longer season. He was also helped by the higher level of players around him.

"The improvement in Joey from the start of his freshman year to that spring was magnificent," said coach Bertman. "When he came here he was a pull hitter, but he learned to hit balls to right field much better. He was driving the ball over the fence. The thing he really benefitted from was the fall season. He had played football in high school and then they had a short baseball season in the spring. When he came to LSU, we practiced 12

In his youth, Belle preferred to be called Joey. Later, trying to change his image of a hard-to-handle player with an explosive temper, he went back to his given name, Albert.

straight weeks in the fall. That's why he grew."

Joey had several big hits as a freshman, including a two-out, two-run homer to beat Mississippi State. That summer he went home and played American Legion ball.

"We went to Arkansas one time for a little tournament and he hit six home runs and a double," said Mike Spence, his Legion coach. "We were playing in a small town and they didn't get to see many college players. A ton of people came out to watch and by the time we left he had people talking."

Among them were some pro scouts. Bertman was quickly building LSU into a national power. During Joey's three years at LSU, he played with future big-leaguers Mark Guthrie, Ben McDonald, Barry Manuel, Jack Voigt, and Jeff Reboulet, among others. With so many excellent players on the team, scouts couldn't help but notice the awesome power-hitting potential of Belle.

Joey became one of the best power hitters in college history. In his three years at LSU, he set school career records in seven offensive categories, including home runs (49), RBI (172), runs (157), hits (194), and slugging percentage (.670). He batted .332 and was all-Southeastern Conference as a sophomore and junior. *Baseball America* named him second-team all-America as a sophomore and third team as a junior.

Scouts loved his commitment to improve, his competitiveness and intensity. They marveled at how such a young player could be so focused on hitting that he'd even study the pitchers warming up in the bullpen. Bertman projected him to be a high first-round pick in the 1987 major league draft of amateur players.

But between his sophomore and junior years, Joey seemed to change—a change so dramatic that Bertman went to Joey's mother and suggested he get counseling. "He wasn't a bad kid. He wasn't robbing stores or stealing cars," Bertman said. "But he always had a temper problem. He would strike out and throw his helmet or bat. He would pop up or top a ball to the pitcher and not run it out. Then, as the scouts started talking to him late in his sophomore and early in his junior years, he got nervous. He got a lot of attention and he didn't know how to handle it."

Bertman would occasionally bench Joey for his temper tantrums. It was a side of the player he could not understand. Joey was well-liked by his teammates, and he spent a lot of time working at the local high schools, signing autographs and visiting sick kids in the hospital. LSU teammate Pete Bush said, "I tell you what: I can promise you, the charity work, the other stuff he does now, it isn't for show. It's from the heart."

But the pressure to succeed may have affected Belle. "It got to the point where he'd strike out and guys in the dugout would be looking at each other and saying, 'I wonder what he's going to hit this time, or what he's going to throw," Bush added.

"The truth of it is, he couldn't control himself," Bertman said.

Bertman benched Joey six times in his junior year for his tantrums. One of those times would be the most critical of his career, and the last time he would play college baseball.

LSU was playing Mississippi State in the 1987 SEC tournament. A Mississippi State fan sitting behind Belle in right field was yelling racial slurs

LSU coach Skip Bertman demanded that his players hustle at all times and have a good attitude. Bertman suspended Belle six times one year, and kept him on the bench while the Tigers lost the 1987 College World Series.

at him. Joey ignored the fan for a while, before finally cracking and racing up the hill after him. His teammates restrained him. But later in the game, Joey failed to run out a long drive to center field. He thought it was a homer, but the ball didn't clear the fence. Instead he got only a single because he didn't hustle.

"He had been told that if he didn't run out a ball again he would be suspended," Bertman said. "Well, he did it again and he was suspended. We played the next day and advanced to the regional playoffs and then went on to the College World Series. He had run out of chances."

Joey was furious. It had been one of his most satisfying years because Terry had been playing left field and designated hitter and they were starting together for the first time since high school. "He made me play so much better," Terry said. "He just made me feel like I could go out in a rowboat with a jar of tartar sauce and catch Moby Dick."

Bertman said it was hard for Joey to sit on the bench in the regionals and College World Series and watch his brother play. And what Bertman's stance did was scare the scouts away from Joey. LSU lost in the World Series semifinals and the scouts wondered if Bertman had cost himself a national championship by benching his best player for the team's most important games.

"There is a time when you have to respect your teammates and respect your game. He couldn't understand that," Bertman said.

The Atlanta Braves decided they would not take Joey in the draft regardless of his skills. General manager Bobby Cox, who later became the Braves' manager, told his scouting director, "If you pick Belle in any round, you're fired."

Other teams concluded that for Bertman to take such a position with so much on the line indicated that Joey lacked respect for his team or the game.

The Cleveland Indians were not concerned about what happened at LSU. In their ranking of draft-eligible players, Ken Griffey, Jr. was first, followed by Belle. When Joey was still available in the second round, Indians' scouting director Jeff Scott said, "I'm not going to run from this kind of talent." Bertman agreed with him and said he thought Joey would grow up.

Joey remained angry at Bertman. He thought the benching cost him being a first-round pick and at least $40,000 in bonus money. Joey's mother handled the contract negotiations with the Indians. The team offered a $50,000 signing bonus, but the Belles wanted $125,000—the amount they figured he would have gotten if he had been drafted in the first round. The two sides argued throughout the summer. Just when the Indians were about to give up, Belle agreed to a bonus of $80,000, and his professional career was under way.

5

A PATTERN OF BEHAVIOR

"People are human beings. Sometimes they can't hold it in any longer, and they have to explode."

— Dennis Martinez, Indians pitcher

The day after he signed his contract, Joey reported to the Indians' minor league team at Kinston, NC in the Class A Carolina League. Just 11 games were left in the season, but on his first day of batting practice, he belted pitch after pitch over the fence. Players from both teams stopped and watched the display.

Belle didn't stay in the minor leagues very long. He split the 1988 season between Kinston and Class AA Waterloo in the Midwest League. In 1989, he was leading the Eastern League at Canton-Akron with 20 home runs and 69 RBI when the Indians brought him up on July 15.

But Belle had not made a good adjustment to being away from the security of his family for the first time. The mistrust of people he had developed in college, and his obsession for perfection, intensified. The self-inflicted pressure to perform mounted. He would tear up the clubhouse with a bat. Once he packed his bags and left the ballpark. He hurled bats and batting helmets after striking out. He was thrown out of the Mexican

On May 13, 1991 Belle reads a written statement to Cleveland fans apologizing for throwing a ball into the stands, hitting a fan in the chest. Belle continued to be involved in similar incidents, resulting in suspensions and fines by league officials.

winter league for throwing a catcher's mask out of the stadium.

But his teammates talked about Belle's good side—of the guy who was witty and pleasant, singing in the clubhouse. They said he was smart, a master of chess and crossword puzzles. He was loyal to teammates and he would often be found in a batting cage at 1 a.m. working on his hitting. He worked with local and national charities, including Big Brothers/Big Sisters, Multiple Sclerosis and the United Way. Later the Indians would twice nominate him for the Roberto Clemente Award, given to the player who best represents baseball on and off the field. He won the Branch Rickey Award for community service.

The Indians' had a dilemma: Belle displayed super talent but erratic behavior. Somehow, Belle seemed to believe that hitting home runs, working hard, and donating time and money excused his behavior. Perhaps it had all begun as far back as Little League. "Joey used one of the bigger bats in Little League and we beat one team so bad that they wanted to protest his bat," said his coach, Gene Procell. "He was actually using a regulation bat—it was just heavier than most—but because it didn't have a Little League label on it they were upset."

From then on, coaches and teammates along the way could recall examples of his temper. A series of incidents, on top of his tantrums in the minor leagues, led the Indians to believe that Belle had an alcohol problem. When he tore the sink off a clubhouse wall and destroyed it with a bat in 1990, the club asked him to enter a clinic for alcohol abuse and get counseling for his temper.

"While in the clinic, I discovered that I have had problems with concentration, motivation, attitude and temper," he said after the two-month stay at the clinic. "I have found a new way of life through the clinic's program and a 12-step recovery plan."

He emerged from the clinic vowing a fresh start. To prove his sincerity he announced that he wished now to be known by his given name of Albert instead of Joey. But many people, including his mother and Coach Bertman at LSU, doubted Belle ever had a drinking problem. They knew he never lacked "concentration" and "motivation"—words he cited as problems before going to the clinic.

"Joey goes along with it because if he doesn't, the Indians will dump him," his mother said at the time. But the Indians had received reports of Belle sitting in his room drinking and sometimes showing up at the park moody and smelling of alcohol. With the time he spent in the clinic, the team believed Belle's problems were cured.

Belle's prominence as a star and his tendency to throw temper tantrums attract constant media attention to him. Belle blames a "smear campaign" by the media for creating his bad-boy image.

After he was released from the clinic, he spent the rest of the 1990 season at Class AAA Colorado Springs and Canton-Akron and stayed with the big-league club in September, though he was not on the roster. Then, during the off-season, the troubles returned.

He was thrown out of the Puerto Rican winter league for not hustling. In 1991, he made the big-league club when he was the spring training leader with 11 homers and 27 RBI in just 23 games. But during the season he got mad at a fan who was yelling at him and threw a baseball that hit the man in the chest. Belle was suspended for a week. He was sent back to Colorado Springs for failing to run out a double play grounder. Despite all of that and playing just 123 games, Belle led the Indians with 28 homers, 95 RBI and 31 doubles.

In 1992, he was suspended for three games for charging the mound against Royals pitcher Neal Heaton. He served another three-game suspension in 1993, when he charged the mound against the Royals' Hipolito Pichardo.

At spring training in 1994, a fan named Joe Plaso was watching a game between the Indians and Tigers and taking photos when a ball zinged off Belle's bat and hit him in the head. Plaso didn't get the foul ball, but he did get 17 stitches to close his wound and a really cool photo of the ball just before it bloodied his head.

A few days later Plaso asked Belle to sign the photo for him, but he refused. The fan was disappointed, yet remained a fan of the controversial slugger.

"I think sometimes our expectations of Albert Belle are best left when he's in the batter's box," he said.

During that season, Belle was suspended for seven games for using a bat filled with cork, which is illegal. The penalty might not have been so bad if some of his teammates had not broken into the umpires' room to steal the bat and replace it with one that was not corked. Instead of putting another model of Belle's bat in the room, they left one of teammate Paul Sorrento's bats. The thieves were caught red-handed. John Kruk of the Philadelphia Phillies said, "He was already hitting the ball 800 feet. I guess he wanted to hit it 1,000."

Belle also made a scene at the 1995 World Series when he swore at TV reporter Hannah Storm and ordered her from the dugout, drawing a $50,000 fine. A few weeks later on Halloween night, some kids knocked on his door for candy. When he told them he had run out, they threw eggs at his house. Belle jumped into his truck and chased after the kids. He drove onto a sidewalk and into a field after them, bumping one of them with the truck.

"As soon as I caught up with him, I slammed on the brakes and was jumping out of the car and was going to run after him," Belle said. "It was raining and it was kind of mucky back there. The truck kind of skidded, or whatever, and it slid and bumped him. He fell down and as soon as he fell down, he jumped back up and started running."

Belle was fined $100 and charged with reckless operation of a vehicle. "People are human beings," said teammate Dennis Martinez. "Sometimes they can't hold it in any longer, and they have to explode."

To the Indians, the scary part of the Halloween incident was the possibility that one of the youngsters might have been injured. They

Cleveland Indians manager Mike Hargrove, in addition to battling umpires, had to defend Belle's outbursts and maintain a calm clubhouse in their wake. "There are things Albert does that nobody in the clubhouse likes or condones," he said. "But he's still one of us, and we will do what we can to help him."

wondered what Belle might have done if he had caught one of them. Would he have done something that would haunt him the rest of his life? Perhaps he was lucky the kids got away.

Belle realized it, too, and during the off-season of 1995-96 he did something he rarely did: he gave interviews. After seeing so many negative stories about his behavior, he had refused to talk to the media for a long time. It was an attitude that would keep him from winning the most valuable player award in 1995, and one that would keep the public from seeing his good side. But because he did not talk to the media, few people knew the good side of Belle. The average fan did not see that the focus, tension and anger Belle displayed during the baseball season gave way to a friendly and caring person off the field. They did not see him

leading the team in prayer, and comforting others when teammates Tim Crews and Steve Olin were killed in a boating accident in the spring of 1993. As a result of his image, whether right or wrong, Belle lost millions of dollars in endorsements.

"I don't think he's happy with his image," his brother said. "I think anybody cares when you take shots at their character, but the only thing he wants is to play baseball. The media situation could be handled better. If I was him, I'd be making $5 million in endorsements off the field. But the main thing is, he's not a villain. He's a nice guy with a great sense of humor."

So during that winter he allowed a few reporters to see the side of his personality that teammates and old friends have long said existed. *The Sporting News* and *USA Today Baseball Weekly* spent time with him on a golf course, where he signed autographs, joked around with fans, and posed for pictures. There were no thrown golf clubs or signs of the intense ballplayer who seemed to battle himself as much as opposing pitchers.

"He's not like that off the field," said New York Mets pitcher Greg McMichael, who played with Belle in the minors and majors. "Some guys have a different game face."

"You're not going to see a side of a guy, like how he reacts with kids and stuff, and at home," Belle said. "You're going to see how this guy reacts at work. Maybe it's good, maybe it's not good. That's all you've got to go by."

"In a foxhole, I'll take Albert," Indians general manager John Hart said. "But you're wasting your time if you're trying to figure him out."

6

CHASING HISTORY

"He could break Roger Maris' record."
— Andre Thornton

Through the first half of the 1990s no cleanup hitter was more dangerous than Albert Belle. He would stand deep in the batter's box and crowd the plate, daring a pitcher to challenge him. "I like to look in a pitcher's eye and see how he feels that day," Belle said. "You can tell if a guy is confident out there, or not confident."

Belle could be so menacing at the plate that some pitchers were afraid to throw him a pitch he could hit. If Belle got a fastball on the inner part of the plate, he would pound it to left field. If he got a breaking ball, he would wait until the last split second and drive it into right field.

"I always thought Albert would hit for a lot of power," said Hall of Famer Frank Robinson. "But he has learned to hit to right field and become a .300 hitter—that has really impressed me."

The rise of the Indians coincided with Belle becoming the regular left fielder in 1992. From 1954 to 1994, Cleveland witnessed some of the worst baseball in history. The Indians did not finish above fourth place from 1969 to 1993. Only four times in that period did they win more games than they lost. Rumors persisted that the team would move to New Orleans, Denver or Tampa.

Belle was especially rough on 5-foot-7 Fernando Vina in 1996, sending the Milwaukee infielder to the hospital with a possible broken nose while breaking up a double play on May 31. A week later Belle flattened Vina with a forearm to the head and drew a two-day suspension.

The Cleveland Indians moved into their new ballpark, Jacobs Field, on April 4, 1994, after playing for decades before mostly empty seats in 80,000-seat Municipal Stadium. Jacobs Field was sold out for the entire season before opening day.

Suddenly, they looked like they were on the edge of greatness and would be playing for the championship for many years. Their rebuilt farm system was allowing them to gradually trade off aging players, and their young and exciting stars such as center fielder Kenny Lofton, right fielder Manny Ramirez, and third baseman Jim Thome gave them a powerful nucleus.

But Belle was the centerpiece of the offense. In 1992, he clubbed seven homers in a nine-game stretch in May, and hit three homers in a game against Texas late in the season. He finished with 34 homers and 112 RBI and the Indians went from last place in 1991 to fourth place.

Belle established himself as one of the game's best run producers in 1993, when his 129 RBI led the American League. But the team never regrouped after the fatal accident to pitchers Olin and Crews, and finished sixth.

Vowing to make a fresh start in 1994, they moved into their new park, beautiful Jacobs Field. Despite the big left field wall and wide-open space in left-center field, Belle managed to place in the top three in 10 American League offensive categories. When the players went on strike August 11 and didn't return the rest of the season, Belle had 36 homers, 101 RBI and a .357 batting average.

"It's amazing," said former Indians slugger Andre Thornton. "I played in a great era of baseball, with guys like Reggie Jackson, Mike Schmidt, Billy Williams and Hank Aaron. But what Albert is doing now exceeds those players."

Said former Indians pitcher Herb Score, one of the team's announcers: "He's so focused that when he walks out to home plate, he probably wouldn't notice if half the ballpark fell down."

In 1995, as the Indians raced toward the American League pennant, Belle became the first player to hit 50 homers and 50 doubles in a season.

"I kind of surprised myself with the 50 home runs," Belle said. "I never thought about it. I thought the [Indians team] record of 43 was attainable, but it seemed like I got into a groove at the end of the year and everything went. I was just trying to hit for a high average, but the home runs started piling up."

The joyous Indians reached the playoffs and defeated the Boston Red Sox in three straight games to advance to the American League Championship Series against the Seattle Mariners. Belle's homer in the 11th inning tied Game 1. But he did not have a good series against the Mariners. He sprained his ankle in Game 3, did not play the next night, and made a costly error in Game 5. He batted just .222 with one homer and RBI in the series. But the Indians advanced to the World Series by winning four games to two because their pitching stopped the Seattle sluggers.

There was great anticipation for the World Series because the strike of 1994 had forced the cancellation of the Series for the first time in 90 years. The powerful Indians met the pitching-rich Atlanta Braves and excitement built around seeing Belle face Atlanta's Greg Maddux, who had won four straight Cy Young awards for being the National League's best pitcher.

A big part of Belle's success was preparation. For months he had been watching Maddux on TV. By the time the World Series began, he had more than 40 tapes of Maddux. Belle also kept notes of pitchers on little index cards.

In Game 1 of the World Series, Belle went hitless as Maddux allowed just two hits and two unearned runs in a 4–3 victory. In Game 2, the Braves used a two-run homer by Javier Lopez to take a 4–3 victory and 2–0 Series lead.

With the Series shifting to Cleveland, the Indians gained some confidence and won Game 3 in 11 innings, 7–6. Belle was struggling at the plate and seemed to be pressing too hard to produce. He finally broke open in Game 4 by hitting a home run, but the Braves moved to within one game of winning the World Series with a 5–2 victory.

Belle had stayed up long nights studying Maddux, preparing for Game 5. With the Indians nearing elimination, the pressure mounted. "I think I have the pitcher thinking when I come up," Belle said. "He better have his best stuff. He may get me once, he may get me twice. But sooner or later, I'll get him."

In the first inning, Belle came to bat with two outs and a runner on base. He crowded the plate and drove Maddux's first pitch over the right field wall for a home run. It ignited the Indians to a 5–4 victory.

The Series shifted back to Atlanta for Game 6 with the Braves still needing just one victory to become world champions. The two teams battled in a scoreless game until the sixth inning, when Atlanta's David Justice hit a solo home run. The Braves' Tom Glavine allowed just one hit, and the 1–0 lead stood up for a Braves' victory and World Series title.

The Indians hit just .179 in the Series; Belle batted .235 with two homers and four RBI. But the nation got a closer look at one of the game's best hitters, the man many believe had the best chance of breaking Roger Maris's record of 61 homers in a season. During the off-season Belle talked openly of Maris's record, saying, "Hitting 60 can be done. It can be done with a lot of luck. Somebody is going to hit .400 or break the home run record, but you've got to have a lot of luck. Maybe before the turn of the century somebody will do it."

But trouble started early for Belle in 1996. During the first week of the season he was accused by a photographer of purposely throwing baseballs at him and cutting his hand. Then a turbulent nine-game road trip at the end of May and early June greatly affected him and the team. In the first series in Detroit, "there were some fans right on top of our dugout that were on Albert unmercifully," said manager Mike Hargrove. "He never blinked, never reacted, never turned around. If it was me, I would have had to go up and visit those guys. But Albert didn't say a thing."

But on the next stop in Texas, Belle cursed at a fan who wanted to exchange Belle's 21st home-run ball for an autographed ball. Belle said he recognized the man from a group of hecklers in the left field seats. Then, three days later in Milwaukee, Belle flattened Brewers second baseman Fernando Vina with a forearm to the head while breaking up a double play.

That incident helped lead to a bench-clearing brawl in the ninth inning. Belle was suspended for five games by the American League, a sentence that was later reduced to two games. The nation's media jumped all over him, calling him a jerk, menace, and villain.

"He is a marvelous, hard-working hitter," wrote Mike Lopresti of Gannett News Service. "There probably is no one who deserves his statistics more. And no one who deserves to hear the cheers of the crowd or enjoy the trappings of popularity less. Albert Belle should hit his homers in an empty stadium."

Early in 1996 it appeared that Belle would threaten the home run record. He had 21 by the end of May, picking up where he left off in 1995. But he had a miserable June, hitting just four homers and batting .222. Then more trouble came. Belle got into a yelling match with a reporter in Chicago. Fans in New York threw two baseballs and a miniature bat at him. He took a bat and destroyed two clubhouse thermostats because he wanted the room a lot colder than his teammates, who began to tire of the tirades and the constant media attention toward his behavior. Even Belle seemed affected by all that was happening around him.

"Sometimes it got a little scary when things started flying around," said Sandy Alomar, Jr.

"But what could you say? The guy is a great hitter."

"There are things Albert does that nobody in the clubhouse likes or condones," said manager Mike Hargrove. "But he's still one of us, and we will do what we can to help him."

"We are tired of seeing the negative things," Belle said. "I can do 100 good things and the one negative thing overshadows all of it. It's something I am going to have to continue to work on. I think the media hasn't focused on what I have done in between the white lines. What I've done outside the lines, maybe it sells newspapers, but all I am really concerned about is staying productive."

Leadoff man Kenny Lofton was a primary factor in the Indians' 1995 pennant-winning season. A Gold Glove center fielder, Lofton led the American League in stolen bases each of his first six seasons.

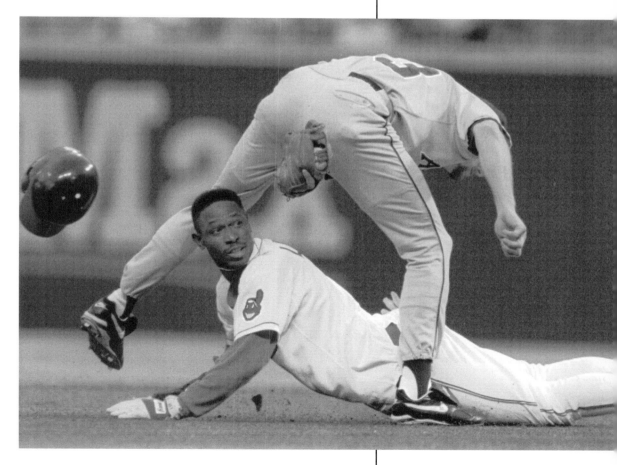

When Belle hits a home run, he gets upset if he doesn't hit it as hard as he wanted. So when he strikes out, as he has just done in Game 2 of the 1995 World Series, his scowl looks even more like a volcano about to erupt.

In July, he was soundly booed at the All-Star Game in Philadelphia. But his bat came alive in the second half of the season and he finished with 48 homers, a .311 batting average and a league-high 148 RBI. The Indians reached the postseason again, but were upset by the Baltimore Orioles in the division playoffs.

With the disappointing postseason, and the distractions and negative publicity surrounding Belle, 1996 ended on a bitter note for Cleveland. But the Indians' players continued to praise Belle.

"He's the best player in baseball," Jim Thome said. "Fans pay to see hitters hit the ball, and that's what Albert does better than anyone. I've been playing with him for five years, and I've never had a single run-in with him. I've never even seen the bad side of him people talk about."

"We pay him to produce, and he does," general manager John Hart said. "I'm not saying he always does the right thing. But if you're expecting me to say something negative, you're not going to hear it."

But before the year ended, Hart was no longer paying Belle to produce.

7

A FITTING END

"Frank [Thomas] wanted Belle—period."
— Jerry Reinsdorf, White Sox owner

For the last 30 years of the 20th century, baseball toiled in a constant battle between its owners and players. The anger and mistrust on each side grew to such a level that either the players went on strike or the owners locked them out seven times. In 1981, a players' strike shut down the game for 51 days. In 1994 a strike canceled the last six months of the season and, for the first time in 90 years, there was no World Series.

The core of the 1994 strike was the players' belief that the owners were trying to drive down salaries, which were averaging nearly $800,000 per player. The bitter talks between the two sides lingered throughout the winter and into the early part of spring training in 1995. Fans disagreed over which side was right. But they could clearly see the game of baseball being ruined by millionaires pleading how poor they were becoming.

When a court order ended the strike, many fans stayed away from the games in protest of the strike. Polls showed basketball and football far ahead of baseball in popularity.

For two years the game continued without a labor agreement. The owners kept proposing a

Despite league president Gene Budig's belief that "Albert Belle has a problem and the American League has a problem" with Belle's behavior, Cleveland fans were solidly behind the slugger, shown here acknowledging their cheers after a home run. But the fans' support did not stop Belle from moving to the Chicago White Sox after the 1996 season.

plan, called a salary cap, that would prevent teams from spending too much money on players. But the players refused to consider it. The most outspoken club owner on limiting salaries was Jerry Reinsdorf, owner of the Chicago White Sox. Chicago was the nation's third-largest city; his team's revenues were much greater than those of teams in smaller markets like Milwaukee, Pittsburgh, and Kansas City. Maintaining that the owners should not give in to the players' demands, Reinsdorf reasoned that salary restraints and revenue sharing would give even the smaller cities a chance to compete for the better players.

No owner had more influence during the strike than Reinsdorf. He took control of meetings and committees, telling the poorer teams that when a deal with the players was finally reached, they would be rewarded. In the meantime, they had to be patient and follow his lead.

Meanwhile, Albert Belle was watching carefully. He would be free to sign with any team at the end of the 1996 season, and he made it no secret that he wanted to top Ken Griffey, Jr.'s $8.5 million annual salary and become the highest-paid player in baseball. The Indians began negotiating with Belle early in 1996, and reportedly offered $7.3 million a year for five years. They later raised their offer to $8.6 million. Belle quickly refused both offers, saying he wanted $9 million a year for six years.

The Indians were aware of their fans' devotion to Belle, and the work he did in the community. He was also the most productive hitter in the game. The team viewed itself as Belle's family, which had come to his rescue time and again. Surely, they believed, he would recognize the comfort zone that had been built around him in Cleveland. Surely, he was not so selfish as to leave a place where he was loved and protected. And they thought their financial offer was more than generous.

When the season ended, there were signs that the players and owners were moving toward an agreement on a plan involving revenue sharing and a tax on team salaries above a certain figure. On November 6, 1996, the owners gathered to vote on a contract that the negotiators from both sides had agreed upon. Influenced by Reinsdorf's opposition, acting commissioner Bud Selig, owner of the Milwaukee Brewers, persuaded the owners to reject the agreement.

Belle's teammates had only good things to say about him, although catcher Sandy Alomar, Jr. admitted, "Sometimes it got a little scary when things started flying around." Here Kenny Lofton (left) and second baseman Carlos Baerga (right) pose with Belle in the last spring training they would enjoy together, in 1996.

Belle poses with new teammate Frank Thomas (right) in Chicago on November 19, 1996, after signing a five-year contract that made him the highest-paid player in history. Belle and Thomas, the most productive run producers of the 1990s, gave the White Sox the most powerful one-two punch in the game.

The public, believing the long-simmering, disruptive feud had ended, was shocked and disgusted when the peace plan was turned down.

Then, two weeks later, Reinsdorf, who had pleaded for salary restraint, shocked the baseball world by signing Belle to a whopping $55 million White Sox contract for five years. Now, with Belle and All-Star Frank Thomas, he had $18 million a year invested in two players, which was more than the entire payroll of four teams.

The smaller teams, including Selig's Milwaukee Brewers, felt betrayed. The game had suffered irreparable harm from the strikes and the owners' hard-line stance against the players. And now their ringleader had done exactly what he had preached against for four years: spending recklessly.

Reinsdorf explained that if he had not signed Belle, some other team would have offered as much. The White Sox had finished 14 1/2 games behind the Indians in the American League Central in 1996. Attendance at Comiskey Park had dwindled to just 21,220 a game. "The more I thought about it and the more I talked to my people," he said, "the more I realized what would most excite our fans and get them back into the ballpark was to do something dramatic."

The other owners were so angry, they called an emergency meeting to take another vote on the labor contract. At the meeting, San Diego Padres president Larry Lucchino said, "Jerry, we've listened to you for four years. You have been on every committee and you've been wrong every time you told us we had to do something. It's time for you to stop talking and get out of the way."

The owners approved the contract, 26–4, guaranteeing peace between the owners and players until the year 2001. Finally, the game could concentrate on the action on the field, not in the courtroom.

Cleveland fans were stunned by Belle's lack of loyalty. One wrote to The Sporting News, "I guess Albert Belle has confirmed what us Cleveland fans tried to repress. This truly is a case of take what's best for Albert and forget what everyone has done for him. Jacobs Field is the only park you've never been 'booed' in. Can't wait to break that bad habit. I hope I'm there when you come to town. Good riddance."

"Going to a new team is like going to a new high school," Belle said. "Nobody knows you. It's a chance to rebuild your image."

In Chicago, Frank Thomas was overjoyed. Thomas, the American League MVP in 1993 and 1994, was a hitter of incredible power and skill, capable of winning the triple crown. But pitchers often walked him, preferring to take their chances with the next man in the lineup. Now, with Belle batting behind him, they would have to pitch to Thomas. The two sluggers could form the most potent power package since the Yankees' Mickey Mantle and Roger Maris in the 1960s.

"Frank wanted Belle—period," Reinsdorf said. "I said to him, 'How about Barry Bonds? I hear he's available.' And Frank said, 'Oh, no. Albert's better. He's the guy I want.'"

Belle was honored by Thomas's praise; part of his decision to go to the White Sox may have been based on comments Thomas had made during the 1996 debate on the MVP Award. "It's all politics," Thomas said of the voting that gave the award to Texas slugger Juan Gonzalez. "The man deserves it. I think it's Albert's turn."

Belle looked forward to the challenge of backing up Thomas in the batting order. "All that stuff—RBI title, batting race, home run race— all of that will take care of itself. I want to come into this situation and produce early on so teams know they can't pitch around Frank Thomas to get to me . . . That's what I want everyone to understand from day one to the last day of the season.

"I love the pressure. People are expecting me and Frank to do these Babe Ruth and Roger Maris-type seasons every year now, which will be fun, but I want to take on all the pressure. If anybody wants to blame anything on the White Sox, just blame it on Albert. It's no problem."

At the age of 30, Belle was in the prime of his career, as a slugger and as the center of controversy. From the time he was in Little League, his complex personality and drive for perfection had angered people. Now, his desire to be the highest-paid player in baseball history had led to the end of the most bitter and destructive labor strife in sports history.

Somehow, it was fitting.

CHRONOLOGY

1966   Born Albert JoJuan Belle August 25 in Shreveport, Louisiana; twin brother Terry is born four minutes later

1984   Graduates sixth in high school class of 266; attends Louisiana State University on baseball scholarship

1987   Drafted by the Cleveland Indians in second round

1989   Makes major league debut July 15 with single in first at-bat off Nolan Ryan; hits first major league home run July 19

1993   Plays in first All-Star Game

1995   Becomes first player to hit 50 doubles and 50 home runs in a season

1996   Becomes highest-paid player in history by signing five-year, $55 million contract with Chicago White Sox

MAJOR LEAGUE STATISTICS

CLEVELAND INDIANS

YEAR	TEAM	G	AB	R	H	2B	3B	HR	RBI	BA	SB
1989	CLE	62	218	22	49	8	4	7	37	.225	2
1990		9	23	1	4	0	0	1	3	.174	0
1991		123	461	60	130	31	2	28	95	.282	3
1992		153	585	81	152	23	1	34	112	.260	8
1993		159	594	93	172	36	3	38	129	.290	23
1994		106	412	90	147	35	2	36	101	.357	9
1995		143	546	121	173	52	1	50	126	.317	5
1996		158	602	124	187	38	3	48	148	.311	11
Totals		913	3441	592	1014	223	16	242	751	.295	61

World Series

1995		6	17	4	4	0	0	2	4	.235	0

FURTHER READING

Bamberger, Michael. "He Thrives on Anger."
Sports Illustrated, May 6, 1996.

Kuenster, John. "Albert Belle's Words and Actions
Dishonored Major League Baseball." *Baseball
Digest*, October 1996.

Johnson, Paul M. "Albert, Can You Talk For—?"
Sport Magazine, November 1996.

Wulf, Steve. "For Him the Belle Toils." *Time,*
December 2, 1996.

Callahan, Gerry. "Double Play." *Sports Illustrated*,
December 9, 1996.

INDEX

PICTURE CREDITS

AP/Wide World Photos: pp. 8, 32, 35, 38, 40, 42, 47, 48, 50, 53, 54, 58; Jim Hudelson: 14, 18, 23; Louisiana State University: 26, 29; National Baseball Library and Archives, Cooperstown, NY: 2, 11; University Microfilms, Inc.: 20, 24

DENNIS R. TUTTLE, a native of Walnut Cove, N.C., began his sportswriting career at age 17 at his hometown paper, the *Winston-Salem Journal*, in 1977. He has also been a writer and editor at the *Cincinnati Enquirer, Austin American-Statesman, Knoxville Journal*, and *Washington Times*. A 1982 graduate of the University of Cincinnati, he is a two-time winner of an Associated Press Sports Editor's Award for sportswriting excellence. His work has appeared in *The Sporting News, USA Today, Baseball Weekly, Baseball America, Inside Sports, Washingtonian*, and *Tuff Stuff* magazines. He authored *Juan Gonzalez* for Chelsea House in 1995. He resides in Cheverly, Maryland.

JIM MURRAY, veteran sports columnist of the *Los Angeles Times*, is one of America's most acclaimed writers. He has been named "America's Best Sportswriter" by the National Association of Sportscasters and Sportswriters 14 times, was awarded the Red Smith Award, and was twice winner of the National Headliner Award. In addition, he was awarded the J. G. Taylor Spink Award in 1987 for "meritorious contributions to baseball writing." With this award came his 1988 induction into the National Baseball Hall of Fame in Cooperstown, New York. In 1990, Jim Murray was awarded the Pulitzer Prize for Commentary.

EARL WEAVER is the winningest manager in the Baltimore Orioles' history by a wide margin. He compiled 1,480 victories in his 17 years at the helm. After managing eight different minor league teams, he was given the chance to lead the Orioles in 1968. Under his leadership the Orioles finished lower than second place in the American League East only four times in 17 years. One of only 12 managers in big league history to have managed in four or more World Series, Earl was named Manager of the Year in 1979. The popular Weaver had his number, 5, retired in 1982, joining Brooks Robinson, Frank Robinson, and Jim Palmer, whose numbers were retired previously. Earl Weaver continues his association with the professional baseball scene by writing, broadcasting, and coaching.